JOURNEY to the MANGER

Barbara T. Rowland

Copyright © 1991 by Abingdon Press

All rights reserved.
The purchase of a copy of this volume for each cast member conveys rights for performance of this work under church sponsorship, provided there is no charge for admission. Except as noted above, no part of this work may be reproduced or transmitted in any form or by any means, electronic or mechanical, including photocopying and recording, or by any information storage or retrieval system, except as may be expressly permitted by the 1976 Copyright Act or in writing from the publisher. Requests for permission should be addressed in writing to Abingdon Press, 201 Eighth Avenue South, Nashville, TN 37203.

Scripture quotations, other than paraphrases, or unless noted KJV (King James Version), are from the Revised Standard Version of the Bible, copyright 1946, 1952, 1971 by the Division of Christian Education of the National Council of Churches of Christ in the U.S.A. Used by permission.

ISBN 0-687-20592-1

MANUFACTURED IN THE UNITED STATES OF AMERICA

Abingdon Press

SYNOPSIS

The play centers on two young persons whose faith needs strengthening, a young man from 650 B.C. and a girl from today. Through John Mark of Bible times, they are able to bend time and meet in Bethlehem the night of Jesus' birth. After their experiences in Bethlehem, John Mark shows them how the Messiah fits into God's plan since the first covenant with Adam.

SET AND PROPS

Very little is required for the set. A backdrop (curtains or flats) is needed to receive the lights and define the area. A small extension may be built on each side of the sanctuary platform to provide the stage left and right acting areas. Ramps to cover steps leading to the platform provide variety in levels. Remove the pulpit and use center stage. If a choir participates, use separate lights for musicians and black them out during acting. Needed are four stools, one table, a manger and a doll, a low stool, and a simulated campfire. Props needed are two grapevine bracelets, a scroll, a kitty stocking, Christmas wrapping, a chili bowl, shepherds' crooks, gifts from the Wise Men, and a stuffed lamb. If Bethlehem people are included, water pots, baskets, and a ball wrapped with cloth will also be necessary.

CAST
(In Order of Appearance)

JOHN MARK, a young man in biblical dress.
LEAH, a Jewish girl about ten years old.
LEMUEL, a Jewish boy about fourteen who doubts the Messiah will come.
FATHER, a Jewish farmer in Old Testament times.
SALLY, an American girl about fourteen who doubts the Christmas story.
TOM, Sally's tormenting kid brother, about nine.
JANE, Sally's little sister, about eight.
MOTHER, typical harried American homemaker at Christmas.

SPECIAL CAST FOR ACT II

PEOPLE OF BETHLEHEM: any number of participants is acceptable and will depend on who wants to be in the Christmas play. See Act II for ways to use them. The people of Bethlehem may be imagined by Sally and Lemuel if casting is a problem. This is an excellent part for church members who are interested but either are unable to speak well or are too young.
ESTHER, the innkeeper's wife and a good-hearted woman.
MARY, a young, pregnant traveler.
JOSEPH, Mary's husband.
JUDE, a shepherd who allowed his nephew to come and watch.
TOLA, another shepherd, either young or older.
PETER, a boy about eight who wants to be a shepherd.
ANGEL, a messenger from God. This person may be joined by an Angel

Chorus if enough participants are available. (The original production used a tall blonde girl, who was joined by four other teenage girls.)
THREE WISE MEN, older men who come with gifts for Jesus.

SPECIAL CAST FOR ACT III

OLD COVENANT REPRESENTATIVES:

ADAM, a man wearing biblical dress, who made a covenant with God.
NOAH, an older man in biblical dress who tells of his covenant.
ABRAHAM, a man of the land who made a covenant.
MOSES, a strong-looking man with a staff.
DAVID, a man dressed as a king.

NEW COVENANT REPRESENTATIVES:

ROMAN WOMAN AND DAUGHTER, who lived through persecution for being Christians. One person, male or female, is permissible in this role.
MEDIEVAL MAN, one who experienced difficult times with hope.
REFORMATION GERMAN YOUNG MAN AND GIRL, a young man worried about conflicting powers whose sister reminds him of true power.
COLONIAL WOMAN, one who went as a missionary to the colonies.
WOMAN (OR MAN) OF TODAY, a present-day Christian who rejoices in the Christ of Christmas.

ACT I

Scene 1

Center stage lights up to reveal a young man dressed in biblical clothes. He is alone and speaks to the audience.

JOHN MARK: The greatest miracle of all time was the birth of God's Son in human flesh. Jesus was fully God and fully human at the same time. Our minds cannot really understand that—faith lies on the other side of reason. But the truth is that the Almighty Creator of the Universe cares enough for us that he made covenants with our representatives after creation. He had a plan to provide us with a Messiah to set us free from sin and death. And he kept his covenants! Jesus Christ is our New Covenant—our way to a relationship with God.

You're thinking, "I know all that. That's why I rushed to make the church Christmas program. All that theological talk is *why* we celebrate Christmas. So, let's get on with it. Cut the preacher talk."

O.K., O.K. But what time is it? What time are you on? *Chronos* keeps our watches and clocks set. It got you here. It's human time. *Kairos* is real time—God's time. It isn't bound by dimensions. When we are in kairos, we are open to a wider world unlimited by ordinary time or space. Enter kairos with me! Oh, yes. I forgot to introduce myself. My name is John

Mark. Remember, I'm the one who went back home on the first missionary journey I made with Paul and my cousin Barnabas. Paul didn't like it. But my faith wasn't strong enough then to take all they took. I can identify with people who cry, "Lord, I believe. Help thou mine unbelief." *(Mark 9:24 KJV)* It's hard to keep your faith at 100 percent all the time.

Because I understand that, I have this great assignment in eternity! Each year about this time, I take two persons whose faith needs strengthening to Bethlehem! Before Christ was born, there were those who wondered and doubted if he would come. And since the miraculous birth people have wondered and doubted if he really came. Let's look into a home in Ramah in the kingdom of Judah. The year is 650 B.C.

(End of Scene 1. Lights out on center stage, on at stage right.)

Scene 2

Lights stage right reveal LEAH, *about ten, holding open a scroll. Upstage of her is an entrance. Two stools, one taller, are downstage.*

LEAH:	*(Shouts)* Lemuel! Lemuel you better get in here! Come on right now!
LEMUEL:	*(Enters upstage)* Leah! Stop yelling at me. You know Mother doesn't like you to shout in the house. *(Holds cluster of grapes from which he eats)* Besides, I'm too tired to hurry. Been picking grapes all day.
LEAH:	*You* know Father said to study your lesson before he comes in and that I could help you. But all you think about is eating! Lucky for you Father is a farmer! Bet you ate half of what you picked today! Now, I'm going to help you with your study.
LEMUEL:	I don't need a *girl* to help me.
LEAH:	Yes you do! Father said I could ask you questions from Uncle Isaiah's scroll. So, let's do it. Ready?
LEMUEL:	*(Sighs. Pulls up shorter stool and sits.)* I guess so. What's first? *(Pops grape in mouth)*
LEAH:	Uh—*(runs finger along scroll)* oh, here it is. Who acts like sheep? *(giggles)*
LEMUEL:	"We all, like sheep, have gone astray; Each of us has turned to his own way; And the Lord has laid on him the iniquity of us all." See? I know that one!
LEAH:	*(Frowns)* Who'd the Lord lay the ini—the bad stuff on, Lemuel?
LEMUEL:	The Messiah. The one who will come to take away the sin of the world. Don't you know anything?
LEAH:	I haven't studied this as much as you! But I remember Uncle Isaiah saying a Messiah would come.

LEMUEL:	Well, that's the one. We've been looking for him for a long time. Hundreds of years. *(Eats grape)* Sometimes I wonder if he'll really ever come.
LEAH:	*(Shocked)* You shouldn't say that! *(rushes to the door and looks out)* Don't let Father hear you say that!
LEMUEL:	*(Restless. Gets up from the stool and moves around.)* I know, I know. But I *do* wonder. I know the prophecies about him. But will they really happen?
LEAH:	You *must* believe. How can you be head of a family someday and teach your children the Torah if you aren't sure you believe it?
LEMUEL:	I know. I know. But we've waited so long. *(Eats grape)* Sometimes I think— (FATHER *enters suddenly upstage. Moves downstage while he speaks.)*
FATHER:	Greetings, my children!
LEAH:	Hello, Father.
LEMUEL:	Father!
FATHER:	Good. I see you are at your lessons. I stayed in the fields later today and your mother has our mutton stew and barley loaves almost ready to eat. Get yourselves settled and I'll read to you from Uncle Isaiah's scroll. I'll ask you questions next time, Lemuel.

(LEAH *stands leaning against him while he reads and* LEMUEL *sits on the shorter stool slightly down left of* FATHER. LEAH *nods against* FATHER's *shoulder.)*

"For to us a child is born,
to us a son is given,
and the government will be on his shoulders.
And he will be called 'Wonderful Counselor,
Mighty God, Everlasting Father, Prince of Peace.'
Of the increase of his government and of peace
there will be no end. He will reign on David's throne
   and over his
Kingdom, establishing and upholding it with justice
and righteousness from that time on and forever."

(FATHER *continues reading but speaks more softly and we hear* LEMUEL's *thought.* LEMUEL *looks straight out over the heads of the audience.* LEAH *looks drowsy leaning against* FATHER.)

FATHER:	"The zeal of the Lord Almighty will accomplish this." (Isa. 9:6, 7)
LEMUEL:	I want to believe. But I wish I *knew* that the Messiah would come. (End of Scene 2. Lights out on stage right, on at center on JOHN MARK.)

Scene 3

JOHN MARK: Lemuel can identify with my problem. "Lord, I believe. Help thou mine unbelief!" See? Now look in with me at a home in *(name of your state)* in the United States. The year is 19(_ _).

(Lights out on JOHN MARK and on at stage left.)

Scene 4

Lights reveal SALLY, JANE, and TOM wrapping Christmas packages at the dining table.

TOM: Don't use all the red ribbon! I need some for Mom's present. *(Reaches for the roll of ribbon SALLY holds.)*

SALLY: Just a minute! You wait till Christmas Eve to wrap all your gifts and expect to have whatever ribbon you want!

TOM: Look who's talking. What are you doing? Dressing for church?

SALLY: Well, this is a little extra something for our choir director. Not my *family* gifts. *(Finishes with the red ribbon and tosses it to him.)*

JANE: Don't fight on Christmas Eve! *(Holds up pet stocking)* Look at Fluffy's stocking! Stuffed full of bad smelling cat treats!

TOM: Don't hang it till the last minute. That cat'll pull the tree down gettin' to it!

MOTHER: *(Enters carrying pot of chili)* Clear a place for this chili, Sally. You children would pick Christmas Eve to wrap presents when we have to eat and get to church for the pageant. Your dad is in the livingroom going over his part right now. Don't know why they think a history professor is the best one to narrate the choir program.

TOM: Well, Mom, I guess it *is* history. But I'm tired of being a shepherd in that pageant. Same old story every year.

MOTHER: Tom! Of course it's the same story. The birth of Jesus is what we celebrate at Christmas! Did you press your costume?

TOM: Aw, Mom! Who ever heard of a shepherd with an *ironed* robe?

MOTHER: I did! You finish your wrapping and march in there and get your costume ready before dinner.

JANE: My choir robe is ready, Mom. I just sing this year. See Fluffy's stocking? Sally, looks like you could do the story at church sometime. You're always reading and making up stories.

SALLY: Well, maybe I can. I like to imagine what's in somebody's mind—how they feel. Think I'll be a writer when I grow up. See? Didn't this turn out pretty? *(Shows MOTHER completed present)*

MOTHER: *(Absently)* Nice, dear. Now, are your angel things ready for the church play? *(Has been helping TOM with wrapping)*

SALLY:	Yes. But I'm tired of the pageant, too. We always do it exactly the same.
TOM:	Wow! Little Miss Perfect feels like I do about it?
SALLY:	*(Starts to him)* You watch your mouth or I'll—
MOTHER:	*(Grabs her)* Now you two stop it. Tom, go get your costume ready. *(TOM exits.)* Sally, it's not like you to talk like that. What's the matter?
SALLY:	*(Sits with a sigh)* Oh, I don't know. Seems like we rush around so celebrating Christmas—I wonder if it's worth it.
JANE:	We have to rush around! There's lots to do! *(Jumps up and exits while speaking)* I've got to find the collar for my choir robe.
MOTHER:	*(Calls after her)* You said it was ready! Oh, dear!
SALLY:	I wonder if it all really happened as we read in Luke? I wish I could be in Bethlehem the night Jesus was born and talk to the people and find out what they thought and felt. See if it's true.
MOTHER:	*(Pats her shoulder)* I think you're just tired. So am I. Let's just get through tonight and then we can rest. Finish clearing the table while I get the dishes. *(MOTHER exits.)*
SALLY:	*(Nods absently to MOTHER's request. Continues to sit at the table. Leans head on her arms.)* I wish I could *be* in Bethlehem tonight. I wish I could *know* that Jesus Christ was born.

(End of Scene 4. Lights out at stage left. As soon as SALLY has time to get to center stage with JOHN MARK and LEMUEL, lights up at center.)

Scene 5

Lights up at center stage to reveal JOHN MARK *in the center with* LEMUEL *slightly down right on the ramp and* SALLY *across from him slightly down left on the ramp. Both look astonished.*

SALLY:	Hey, what's happening?
LEMUEL:	Where am I?
SALLY:	*(To LEMUEL)* Who are you? *(To JOHN MARK)* And you?
LEMUEL:	I don't know either of *you!* Your garments are strange. Your voice sounds like my sister. But I've never seen male or female dressed like that!
SALLY:	You should talk! You look like somebody right out of a Sunday school book. *(To JOHN MARK)* And so do you!
LEMUEL:	Where are we?
JOHN MARK:	*(Amused at their dismay)* What matters is not where you are *now,* but where you are *going* tonight. But first—introductions. I am John Mark. I lived on your earth once and I know what it's like to question your faith. Sally, meet Lemuel from Judah in 650

	B.C.—he lives under the Old Covenant. And Lemuel, meet Sally from a country across the sea and a time far removed from you. She is under the New Covenant.
SALLY:	Wow! Is this a real time warp like in the movies?
LEMUEL:	A what?
JOHN MARK:	Time—folds together like tablets. It can touch any place. Tonight you go together where you wished to go—the birthplace of the Messiah!
SALLY:	Bethlehem?
LEMUEL:	Where?
JOHN MARK:	*(Takes their arms)* We're going to that *time* when God entered human flesh and to that *place* where the Messiah was born!
	(Holding their arms, JOHN MARK *rushes* SALLY *and* LEMUEL *off stage and down the aisle to exit at back. End of Act I.)*

ACT II

Scene 1

The town of Bethlehem comes to life as lights go up on the second act. The director may use any number of people who want to be in the play. Following is a suggested outline. The original production used three teenage girls for water women; a man and two young persons for travelers; elementary-school-age girls for hopscotch players; a woman with three small girls for shoppers; teenage girls and two small children for ballplayers. The scene may begin in pantomime during music if the play is produced with choir music or congregational singing between acts.

WOMEN GOING FOR WATER:	*(Come down the aisle toward steps with water containers on their head. They climb ramp and cross toward the other side where they meet* TRAVELERS *at the top of stage left ramp.)*
TRAVELERS:	*(Come down side aisle toward stage, beginning after the* WOMEN. *They meet at top of the ramp. In pantomime, they ask for directions to the Inn.* WOMAN *points and all nod.* TRAVELERS *proceed to the inn stage right.* WOMEN *watch.)*
HOPSCOTCH PLAYERS:	*(As* TRAVELERS *go to the inn, these enter stage left and proceed up ramp to down center. They begin to play as if drawing in place. After* ESTHER *turns away the* TRAVELERS, *they go down stage right ramp and watch the game.* GIRL *asks her* FATHER *if she can play, in pantomime unless music is finished. He indicates they must look for lodgings.)*
SHOPPERS WITH BASKETS:	*(Enter stage right and up the ramp as* TRAVELERS *exit. They stop to watch the game. A* GIRL *puts down basket and joins the game.* MOTHER *holds on to the other two children.)*
BALL-PLAYERS:	*(Enter from door stage left. Eager to get outside. One runs onto the ramp and tosses the ball back. Both try to get it. They play awhile.)*
WOMEN WITH WATER:	*(One says, "Come. With all our guests, this water is needed at home."* BALLPLAYERS *exit off stage left.)*

SHOPPERS WITH BASKETS:	*(MOTHER retrieves child from the game of hopscotch. She says,* "We need to get home. Aunt Martha and Uncle Luke will arrive soon." *She begins to exit down stage-left ramp.)*
JOHN MARK, LEMUEL, SALLY:	*(Enter stage left and up the ramp as* SHOPPERS *go down the ramp. They watch as* HOPSCOTCH PLAYERS *conclude the game and exit at stage right. One player says,* "We better go home now. Mother will have our meal ready. With our cousins here, we'll have something good! Come on.")
SALLY:	Ohhhh. Looks like our Christmas pageant—only better costumes!
	(BALLPLAYERS are gathered by older person with them and taken inside through the door stage left.)
LEMUEL:	Hmmm. I smell something cooking. Wonder what they eat here?
JOHN MARK:	I will leave you here in Bethlehem. The Innkeeper will take you as extra help, for the town is crowded.
SALLY:	I know! The census.
LEMUEL:	The what?
SALLY:	Don't you remember? Caesar Augustus wanted to tax the people in the Roman Empire and everybody had to go to his hometown to be registered.
JOHN MARK:	Lemuel can't know about that, Sally. It hadn't happened yet in his time. Now, listen to me for a minute. You two can talk freely with each other. Learn all you can from the evening's events. But say nothing to the people of Bethlehem about your being from another time.
LEMUEL:	*(Nods)* We understand. Where's the inn?
JOHN MARK:	*(Points)* Over there. Go make yourself known. *(Exits quickly)*
SALLY:	*(To center)* Come on. We want to be sure we're there when Mary and Joseph arrive.
LEMUEL:	*(Stops her center stage)* Who?
SALLY:	Mary and Joseph. They come to the inn before the baby is born.
LEMUEL:	The Son of God? Born here! I thought it would be in a palace. But the place *is* right—Micah said, "But you, Bethlehem Ephrathah *[EF ray thah]* though you are small among the clans of Judah, out of you will come for me one who will be ruler over Israel." *(Mic. 5:2)*
SALLY:	Say, is that right? I didn't know you knew *where* in Old Testament days. Come on. *(They go to the inn door and pantomime knock. The Innkeeper's wife,* ESTHER, *comes to the door and pantomimes opening it.)*
ESTHER:	Sorry. Our rooms are full. *(Turns away)*

SALLY: Wait! We've been sent to help you tonight because your inn is full.

LEMUEL: I'll keep your fires going.

ESTHER: Oh! That's different. I could use some help. Come in and get busy. You, girl, stir the soup and you, lad, lay more wood on the fire. I can use a break. *(LEMUEL and SALLY pantomime action and ESTHER sits on a stool.)* My husband is so excited the inn is overflowing, but I'm the one who has to do the work. And no children to help me, either. *(Sadly)* He hates to turn anybody away. But I say we can't help what the Romans order. We can't take care of everybody!

SALLY: What about outside? Is there any room in the caves where you keep the animals?

LEMUEL: For people? Especially for—*(catches himself)*

ESTHER: Well, I never thought of putting people in the—(JOSEPH *and* MARY *enter up ramp stage left and come to the inn door.* JOSEPH *pantomimes a knock at the end of* ESTHER's *line.)*

SALLY: *(Excitedly)* Someone's at the door!

(All three go to the door. ESTHER *opens it.)*

ESTHER: Our rooms are all taken.

JOSEPH: But, my wife is about to have a baby. I must find a place for her. We have our provisions on our donkey at the foot of the hill. Please, isn't there a place we could be safe and warm?

(ESTHER looks at MARY and their eyes lock. ESTHER bites her lip in consternation.)

SALLY: *(Loud whisper to ESTHER)* What about the stall? It would be warm and safe.

LEMUEL: But she's going to have a baby!

ESTHER: *(Lifts her chin with sudden decisiveness)* Yes! You may stay in the animal stall. I'll see there is a clean area and get fresh hay to put under your bedding. *(Turns to SALLY and LEMUEL)* Help these travelers get warm and give them a bowl of soup while I prepare a place for them.

(ESTHER ushers in MARY and JOSEPH. SALLY shows them to the fire. She offers MARY a stool and JOSEPH stands beside MARY. LEMUEL puts log on the fire and SALLY pantomimes pouring soup into a cup and gives to each. Hands one to LEMUEL. ESTHER exits up right.)

SALLY: *(Shyly to MARY as she hands her a cup)* I'm Sally. May I ask your name?

MARY: It's Mary and this is my husband, Joseph. We've come from Nazareth for the census. Bethlehem is Joseph's ancestral home for he is of the house and lineage of David.

LEMUEL: *(With awe)* "Of the increase of his government and of peace there will be no end, upon the *throne of David,* and over his

	kingdom, to establish it, and to uphold it with justice and with righteousness from this time forth and for evermore." *(Isa. 9:7)*
JOSEPH:	You have been well taught, young man.
SALLY:	Did—excuse me—but did anything unusual happen with this pregnancy? *(Kneels beside* MARY *and listens intently)*
MARY:	*(Glances at* JOSEPH *and then speaks)* Oh, yes. An angel told me I would conceive and bear a son. And the angel spoke when Joseph and I were betrothed but not yet married. The angels said, "The Lord God will give him the throne of his father David, and he will reign over the house of Jacob forever; his kingdom will never end." *(Luke 1:32-33)*
LEMUEL:	*(Excited)* Just like the verse I said!
MARY:	Yes. And the angel said the Holy Baby will be called the Son of God—for he is to be born to a virgin through the power of the Most High God.
SALLY:	Weren't you real scared?
MARY:	*(Smiles)* Well, I was thrilled to be chosen to bear God's Son. But I was scared whether or not Joseph would believe me!
LEMUEL:	Did you? What did you think?
JOSEPH:	At first I was numb with disbelief. I knew the Messiah would come someday. But not to my Mary! I was in shock. Then anger replaced the shock. I decided she had betrayed me.
LEMUEL:	You could have had her stoned. Or sent away!
JOSEPH:	Yes. Or marry her quickly and pretend the child was mine.
SALLY:	*(Shocked)* So that's what you did?
JOSEPH:	*(Smiles in memory)* No. That night as I lay on my bed a messenger from God came to me. I felt a Presence and there was a light so intense I had to shield my eyes. A voice told me to be calm and not to fear to take Mary as my wife for that which was conceived in her was of the Holy Spirit.
LEMUEL:	Uncle Isaiah said it! "Therefore the Lord himself will give you a sign: The virgin will be with child and will give birth to a son, and will call him Immanuel." *(Isa. 7:14)*
SALLY:	So you knew it was true! *(Happily)*
JOSEPH:	Yes. *(Arm around* MARY*)* And now the time is almost here for the child to be born. (ESTHER *rushes in.*)
ESTHER:	There is a place for you now. Come with me and I will show you.
JOSEPH:	You may come to us later. Thank you for the soup and warm fire. Good night.
LEMUEL and SALLY:	Good night. (MARY, JOSEPH, *and* ESTHER *exit.*)
LEMUEL:	This *could* all be a big coincidence.

SALLY:	Quick. We must go to the hillside and find the shepherds!
LEMUEL:	Shepherds! Are you crazy?
SALLY:	Come on! (SALLY *grabs his arm and they exit quickly down the ramp and up the aisle to back of the sanctuary.* SALLY *explains—in pantomime—about the shepherds. They prepare to come up the next aisle to enter the hillside scene.*)
	(*End of Scene 1. Lights out on stage right, up half at stage left to reveal three shepherds, two men and a young boy. The boy,* PETER, *holds a lamb. The two men,* JUDE *and* TOLA, *stand by a fire upstage of* PETER.)

Scene 2

PETER:	(*Looking at lamb wrapped in his outer cloak*) The lamb is asleep, Uncle Jude.
JUDE:	Good. He was too little to keep up today. We'll find his mother directly.
TOLA:	Was a good night for you to come along, Peter. You'll take good care of the little one.
PETER:	Oh, yes! I did have to beg Mother to let me come. She thinks it's dangerous out here. (*Looks up*) It's such a beautiful night! So clear.
JUDE:	You can always see better up in the hills.
TOLA:	(*Steps downstage*) Look at Bethlehem. The moon is bright enough to see the village.
JUDE:	Lots of people bedded down there tonight. Caesar's census sure brought a crowd.
PETER:	That's a huge star! See Uncle Jude?
JUDE:	(*Steps forward*) Brightest I've ever seen.
TOLA:	Someone's coming up the hill! (*Motions toward* LEMUEL *and* SALLY *as they approach from the aisle*) Looks like two people. Thought all the shepherds were settled with their flocks by now.
JUDE:	Wonder what they want?
	(LEMUEL *and* SALLY *approach the shepherds.*)
SALLY:	Good evening. Uh—we just—well, we wanted to watch with you awhile if that's all right.
LEMUEL:	We wanted to look down on the village from here. We've never seen Bethlehem at night from the hills.
TOLA:	You shouldn't have come out here alone. But you better stay with us now and be safe.
JUDE:	You watch with Peter here. He has a lamb to show you. I'll get our fig cakes. You may have some.
LEMUEL:	Of course you'd bring food up here. Good. I mean, thanks!
	(JUDE *and* TOLA *step upstage as* LEMUEL *and* SALLY *join* PETER. *All three sit on the platform edge. He shows them the lamb.*)

PETER:	See? The little one is asleep. *(He is between* LEMUEL *and* SALLY *with* SALLY *toward center.)*
SALLY:	Oh! He's so cute. We have sheep near my home. Lots of them. But I never held a little lamb.
PETER:	You live around here?
SALLY:	No—oh—I—well, it's not too far.
LEMUEL:	Do you come up here every night?
PETER:	No. This is a special treat because it's my birthday. I'll be a shepherd when I'm a little older.
JUDE:	*(Steps downstage and hands* PETER, LEMUEL, *and* SALLY *a fig cake)* Here's some fig cake. *(All thank him and take the cake. They settle on hillside.)*
PETER:	I'm glad you came. Even though I wanted to come here, I began to think it might be a long night!
LEMUEL:	Do you sit here all night?
PETER:	Well, I made grapevine bracelets for a while. *(Reaches inside his outer garment and brings out bracelets)* See? You get the vine wet and wrap it around. Take one. *(Hands one to* LEMUEL *and* SALLY. *They thank him and put them on.)*
SALLY:	That's real special, Peter! We'll remember our visit with you on the hillside by the bracelet!
PETER:	*(To* SALLY*)* You want to hold the lamb?
SALLY:	May I? Yes.
	(As PETER *and* SALLY *start to transfer the lamb, suddenly the lights go up bright on stage left and spotlight hits* ANGEL *or* ANGEL CHORUS.*)*
JUDE:	What's happening?
TOLA:	Where's the light—
PETER:	I'm scared!
LEMUEL:	What's goin' on?
SALLY:	It's the Angel!
	(All five lines above said at about the same time. The five actors fall to their knees—four in fright and SALLY *in reverence. The* ANGEL *speaks from elevated platform across from the shepherds.)*
ANGEL:	"Fear not: for, behold, I bring you good tidings of great joy, which shall be to all people. For unto you is born this day in the city of David a Saviour, which is Christ the Lord. And this shall be a sign unto you; Ye shall find the babe wrapped in swaddling clothes, lying in a manger." *(Luke 2:10-12 KJV)*
	(Four additional ANGELS *are with her. Join on verse 14.)*
ANGELS:	"Glory to God in the highest, and on earth peace, good will toward men." *(Luke 2:14 KJV)*
	(Spotlight goes off when ANGELS *finish. Lights up at half of stage left.)*

JUDE:	Let's go to Bethlehem!
TOLA:	We must see what has happened.
LEMUEL:	*(Awed)* The Lord told us about the birth.
PETER:	Uncle Jude, may I take the baby lamb?
JUDE:	Yes, Peter. I'll ask Nathan to watch our sheepfold until we get back.
SALLY:	*(To* PETER*)* Take the baby lamb to see the baby Jesus! And we'll tell Mary what the Angel said!

(End of Scene 2. Lights out at stage left. SHEPHERDS *leave the stage down the ramp and go to the side of stage left. Immediately* MARY *and* JOSEPH *enter in darkness from stage right and take their place up center. The manger with baby and a stool for* MARY *is carried on. As soon as this is in place, lights up at center stage and shepherds approach.)*

Scene 3

PETER:	*(In front)* Look! There's a baby in a manger! Maybe this is the place!
SALLY:	It is! I know it is!
LEMUEL:	That's the couple we met at the inn—
JUDE:	Step back. Let me speak.
TOLA:	Wait with me. *(Puts arms around the young people and stops short of the manger as* JUDE *continues to approach.)*
JUDE:	*(Kneels beside* MARY, *who turns to look at him)* Forgive us for coming to you at night. And when the infant is so newly born. But an Angel told us the Messiah was born in the city of David tonight and that we would find him in a manger.
JOSEPH:	An Angel spoke to you?
JUDE:	Yes. As we tended our sheep on the hillside.
JOSEPH:	Was there a very bright light?
JUDE:	So bright we fell to the ground in fear.
MARY:	So it was with me. An Angel told me the baby I would bear while still a virgin would be the Son of God. This is the Child you seek.
JOSEPH:	Tell the others to come see the Babe.
JUDE:	*(Stands and turns to the other shepherds)* Come and kneel before the new King of Israel!

(The others come forward reverently and kneel. Shepherds are on stage left of MARY. LEMUEL *and* SALLY *kneel stage right of her.)*

JOSEPH:	Greetings to all of you. Mary and I are glad the Angel told to you the truth about our Baby. He is God in human flesh. He *is* the long-awaited Messiah.

MARY: *(Recognizes* LEMUEL *and* SALLY*)* You are the young people who cared for us earlier at the inn! The soup and warm fire gave us strength. I'm glad you came to see the Baby. His name is Jesus.

TOLA: The announcement was so sudden—it all happened so quickly—we have no gifts for the child.

JUDE: We hurried as fast as we could to get here—no thought did we give to . . .

SALLY: He wants our devotion—our belief in him . . .

LEMUEL: I never thought he would come in this manner . . .

PETER: Uncle Jude, may I give baby Jesus the little lamb?

JUDE: Of course, Peter. Give him the lamb.

(PETER carefully places the lamb beside the manger and leans over to pat the baby).

SALLY: Please, may I kiss the baby Jesus?

MARY: Yes. Be careful not to waken him. *(SALLY kisses the baby.)* Now glorify God because he has sent his Son!

JOSEPH: And tell everyone what the Angel said to you about the Child.

JUDE: We must get back to the sheep. *(To* MARY*)* We are honored to see the Child.

MARY: I will keep in my heart the things you have told me this night.

(Lights out at center. Shepherds exit down the ramp at stage left. SALLY and LEMUEL move to stage right acting area. Lights up on them. End of Scene 3.)

Scene 4

LEMUEL: Were the shepherds the only ones who knew the night the Messiah was born?

SALLY: No. There were some Wise Men in the East—Persia I think—who saw the great Star. God broke through their studies somehow to let them know that it was the Star of the new King of Israel.

LEMUEL: But they didn't believe it?

SALLY: Oh, yes, they did. It took them a long time to get here because they came hundreds of miles.

LEMUEL: So Mary and Joseph had gone?

SALLY: No. They stayed in Bethlehem for quite a while. I think Jesus was about two when they left. But we'll get to see the Wise Men since we're bending time anyway. They're always part of Christmas pageants. I want to talk to them!

LEMUEL: So do I!

SALLY: Lemuel! Look!

(SALLY *gestures toward* WISE MEN, *who approach the manger. Lights up on manger and* WISE MEN *just before* SALLY *speaks.* MARY *holds the babe as if he's a small child now. The manger is behind her.* WISE MEN ONE *and* TWO *go to stage left and* WISE MAN THREE *goes to stage right side.* SALLY *and* LEMUEL *move in with him. Lights out on stage right acting area. End of Scene 4.)*

Scene 5

FIRST WISE MAN: *(Kneels)* This must be the Child born King of the Jews.

SECOND WISE MAN: *(Kneels)* We saw his star and came to worship him.

THIRD WISE MAN: *(Kneels)* And we brought gifts—gold, and frankincense, and myrrh. *(They place gifts by the manger.)*

JOSEPH: We are honored you recognized the star and came. Did you have difficulty finding us?

FIRST WISE MAN: We went first to Jerusalem and asked of Herod where to find the new king.

SECOND WISE MAN: Naturally, we thought he would be in a palace.

THIRD WISE MAN: Herod sent for his teachers of the law who knew the prophecy that the Messiah would be born in Bethlehem.

FIRST WISE MAN: Herod told us to let him know if we found the Child so that he could come and worship him. But we were warned in a dream not to tell him for he wants no other king.

SECOND WISE MAN: We'll return another way and not go back through Jerusalem. Herod is jealous and would kill the infant.

MARY: *(Clutches Child)* Oh! I'm so glad you were warned! Don't let him know! And thank you for the wondrous gifts.

JOSEPH: Thank you for coming. Tell the people in your land the promise of God is fulfilled in Bethlehem.

(As the WISE MEN *stand and prepare to leave,* LEMUEL *moves in to the right of* THIRD WISE MAN. SALLY *is to the right of* JOSEPH.*)*

LEMUEL: Pardon me, Wise Men of the East, may I ask a question? *(*THIRD WISE MAN, *standing by him, inclines his head in affirmation.)* Did you know the Jewish Messiah was expected to come?

THIRD WISE MAN: Indeed we did. Even our Persian prophet Avesta told us of one who would arise and make life everlasting.

FIRST WISE MAN: And Balaam, the son of Beor said, "There shall come a Star out of Jacob, and a Sceptre shall rise out of Israel." *(Num. 24:17 KJV; BAY lum, BEE or)*

SECOND WISE MAN:	Your Daniel told us in mystic numbers when he would be born. And we knew he would be King not of the Jews only but of the Gentiles also. We have been watching for a sign. When it came, God made it known to us. *(Dan. 9:25)*
SALLY:	Made it *known.* That must be how we learn spiritual things. God makes it *known*—there is a *knowing*—that we cannot explain! Then we can *come* and *worship!*

(End of Act II. Lights out. Cast exits. Manger is covered with cloth. A tall stool is placed in front of the manger.)

ACT III

Scene 1

Lights up at center stage to reveal JOHN MARK, LEMUEL, *and* SALLY. *Costumes are from the first act. A stool is up at center. We don't see the manger.* OLD COVENANT REPRESENTATIVES *are grouped stage right in darkness.* NEW COVENANT REPRESENTATIVES *are on stage left in darkness.* JOHN MARK *is at center.* SALLY *and* LEMUEL *are on either side and downstage slightly on ramps.*

JOHN MARK:	The greatest miracle of all time is the birth of God's Son in human flesh.
SALLY:	We saw the miracle! We talked to Mary and Joseph and the shepherds!
LEMUEL:	And the Wise Men from the East! We bowed before the infant Messiah! *(Awed)*
JOHN MARK:	And was your faith strengthened? Your unbelief helped?
SALLY:	Yes!
LEMUEL:	Oh, yes!
SALLY:	Lemuel, before we part I must tell you what happened when Jesus grew up—
LEMUEL:	Did he defeat the Romans and rule the world?
JOHN MARK:	He became the bridge between sinful humans and a just God—the Mediator of the New Covenant.
LEMUEL:	What was that?
SALLY:	*That* was church talk. I'll tell you about it. See, Jesus grew up and preached that the kingdom of God is in the hearts of people. He said to love God with all our hearts and love other people as ourselves.
LEMUEL:	So all the people started loving one another?
JOHN MARK:	Unfortunately, no. Many followed him and his teachings. But religious leaders who didn't believe him stirred up the people against him. There was a mockery of a trial and he was crucified on a cross outside Jerusalem.
LEMUEL:	That can't be true! He was God in man. You can't kill God.

SALLY: But Jesus was willing to die as part of God's plan. See, his death paid for the sins of those who accept him as God's Son.

LEMUEL: Like our blood sacrifices? Always there is a blood sacrifice—lamb or something—for payment of sins—under what you call the Old Covenant.

JOHN MARK: That's right. "For all have sinned, and come short of the glory of God" *(Rom. 3:23 KJV)*, and if we "Believe on the Lord Jesus Christ we shall be saved." *(Acts 16:31)*

LEMUEL: It's just like that lesson I learned from Uncle Isaiah: "All we like sheep have gone astray; We have turned each to his own way; and the Lord has laid on him the iniquity of us all." *(Isa. 53:6)*

SALLY: But the best part you don't know yet! Jesus rose from the dead the third day! He is alive!

LEMUEL: Praise the Lord!

SALLY: May we go home now? I can't wait to tell my family about my night in Bethlehem!

JOHN MARK: Before you go, I want you to see the big picture. Hear covenants the all-powerful, Holy God made with sinful, imperfect humans—and how he kept his word. *(Gestures for them to sit)* First, there was Adam. *(JOHN MARK sits on stool. The three actors focus on stage right, where the Old Testament characters enter, speak, and take positions so as to form a chronological line from ADAM to DAVID. David stands nearest the manger area. They address SALLY and LEMUEL.)*

ADAM: I had a covenant with God. He didn't break it. I did. He said for me to populate the earth, rule over the animal creations, care for the garden, and enjoy its fruit. All I had to do was obey him. He gave me the world! But I chose to direct my own path. To take charge myself. To look out for number one and not be committed to my Creator. *(Hangs head)* Then we had to have another covenant. It's the one that sets forth the conditions until the curse of sin is lifted. It's the one that says we die spiritually by sinning and we die physically. Dust to dust. But a Messiah is promised to take away sin!

SALLY: Wow. That long ago God promised a Savior! *(ADAM moves down right on ramp.)*

JOHN MARK: After the covenant with humankind was made with Adam as our representative, came the covenant with Noah.

NOAH: *(Enters as JOHN MARK speaks and is ready to speak.)* When the water went down after the big flood, there were just the eight of us—my wife and I, our three sons and their wives—and God told us to populate the earth. Same conditions he gave Adam plus a principle of government to keep violence in check. He promised never to destroy the earth by flood again. The rainbow is a testimony of his covenant with me.

LEMUEL: I always think of you, Noah, when I see a rainbow.

JOHN MARK: Thank you, Noah. *(NOAH moves down right next to ADAM.)* Next came the covenant with Abraham.

ABRAHAM: God told me to go to a land he would show me. It turned out to be Canaan. And the Lord made a glorious covenant with me! He obligated himself to bring several promised blessings. Said he would make of me a great nation! Would bless my name and make it great! And that all the families of the earth would be blessed through me! What joy! Through my family would come the Messiah!

SALLY: You had no idea how long it would be before he came.

JOHN MARK: You certainly didn't, did you Abraham. *(ABRAHAM smiles and shakes his head negative as he moves away.)* About 430 years later came the covenant with Moses. It was added so that the people of Israel would know how to conduct themselves until the Christ came.

MOSES: *(Enters as JOHN MARK speaks)* The covenant of law given through me to the people of Israel governs our lives as we relate to God and other people. It didn't replace any other covenant. It was added, not so that we could be saved by it but really so that we could realize we can't live perfect lives even with stone tablets to tell us how. We need the sacrifice of the Messiah to have a relationship with a righteous God.

LEMUEL: I memorized those commandments, Moses. But I can't keep them perfectly.

(MOSES shakes his head and moves to his place.)

JOHN MARK: No one can, Lemuel. Thank you, Moses. David is the last representative of the old covenants. About 450 years after Moses, God promised to David a dynasty through which his Son would be born.

DAVID: *(Enters as JOHN MARK speaks)* God promised me a land, a dynasty, and a kingdom forever. He said to me, "When the Messiah comes, he will be of the house of David!" Blessed am I before God!

SALLY: And that's how it happened! God always keeps his promises.

JOHN MARK: Yes, Sally, he does. After King David, the prophet Jeremiah pointed to the New Covenant. And the people looked toward the coming Messiah, who would take away the sins of the world and give faith, hope, and joy to the people of earth.

LEMUEL: Now that we know he came, tell us what happened after he died and rose again.

SALLY: Oh, yes. Let's look at that!

JOHN MARK: Well, the Roman world was turned upside down by the followers of Christ after his resurrection. Paul and other disciples took the Good News of salvation through Jesus and spread it throughout the known world.

(All on stage focus on stage left now. As JOHN MARK speaks, New Covenant Representatives enter and get in place to speak. As each

person finishes, he or she moves to position, so that a chronological line from the Romans of Jesus' day down to the present is formed toward down left.)

ROMAN WOMAN OR MAN: We believers in the third and fourth centuries after Christ need strong faith to meet for worship. The Romans persecuted us and the only safe place to gather was in the catacombs. Roman law said burial places were sacred.

DAUGHTER: It was scary! But we kept our thoughts on Jesus and what he did for us. That gave us courage. We just couldn't give up our worship.

ROMAN WOMAN OR MAN: In spite of all the Roman authorities could do to stop it, the truth of Jesus the Christ—the Messiah—spread! Jews and Gentiles believed. They called us—Christians.

LEMUEL: Gentiles believed, too? Jesus truly came for all people.

JOHN MARK: Yes, he did. Nearly 1,000 years later, Christianity continued to gain believers and to give hope as well as faith.

MEDIEVAL MAN: Because of the holy birth in Bethlehem, Christians through the centuries have hope—for the future in this life and beyond this earth. Our world in the Middle Ages was torn by invasions, disorder, the Black Death devastation, and famine. Our faith in a Messiah who is as alive today as when he came to earth as a Babe in Bethlehem gave us hope.

SALLY: Ohhhh. I read in history about all the terrible things that happened then.

JOHN MARK: During the time of the Renaissance, about the fourteenth and into the seventeenth centuries, came the Reformation. In the sixteenth century, families, churches, and countries split over the issues raised by Martin Luther.

SALLY: All those awful religious wars.

LEMUEL: Nothing new. We had them, too.

GERMAN YOUNG MAN: It's a terrible war here in Germany and fought in the name of God! How far away we get from Jesus' teaching to love God and our fellows. The world is a confusing place to me.

GERMAN GIRL: But no power on earth can touch the power of God. There's no other lasting power. You know Jesus died and rose again so that we could know God—and our sins be forgiven.

GERMAN YOUNG MAN: Of course. God will guide me if I ask him in Jesus' name! My allegiance is to him rather than to any earthly powers.

SALLY: Christians haven't always agreed, have they?

(GERMAN YOUNG MAN and GIRL shake their heads and move away.)

LEMUEL: No! And the world must keep getting bigger. I have never heard of Germany.

JOHN MARK: Nor have you heard of the United States of America. It's across an ocean and was settled by people fleeing religious persecution. In the 1770s a series of revivals called The Great Awakening strongly influenced Americans.

COLONIAL WOMAN: George Whitefield's visit here in Boston made a difference in hundreds of lives. He preached about our individual decision to accept Jesus Christ as God's Son. He made us realize the urgency of taking the Good News to the territories where there were no preachers. My husband and I decided to leave Boston and go West as missionaries.

SALLY: I'm so glad you did! You may have come to my state!

(COLONIAL WOMAN smiles and moves to her place.)

LEMUEL: The news of the Messiah born as a baby in Bethlehem traveled the world!

JOHN MARK: And still travels. Never in history did one life make so much difference in the world. Now, almost 2,000 years since that night in Bethlehem . . .

WOMAN (OR MAN) OF TODAY: *(Enters and takes place as JOHN MARK speaks)* We remember the birth of Jesus with our Christmas celebration each year. Surrounded with traditions, family gatherings, gift exchanges, and feasting—we realize that the manger is overshadowed at times. But we know the life Christ came to give us may be accepted or renewed at Christmas. It's a glorious time when we celebrate the birth of our Savior!

JOHN MARK: The greatest miracle—Almighty God in the baby Jesus—the greatest miracle of all time!

(End of Scene 1. Lights out at center stage area. People in chronological line who are in front of the side stages must sit. Lights up at stage right as soon as LEMUEL has time to get in place. Scene looks exactly as it did when we last saw it in Act I with FATHER, LEAH, and LEMUEL.)

Scene 2

LEMUEL, FATHER, *and* LEAH *are in the same position as in Act I.*

FATHER: *(Closes scroll)* Now. That's enough for this evening. It's time for dinner. *(LEMUEL looks surprised. Stretches as if to throw off sleep and extends an arm in front of FATHER and toward LEAH.)*

LEAH: *(Grabs his arm)* What's this? Looks like you *played* with grapevines instead of picking grapes.

(LEMUEL looks at the bracelet given him by the shepherd boy. FATHER shakes his head. LEAH smirks as if she has caught him in mischief. LEMUEL is astonished. Looks out over the audience. Actors freeze. Lights out. End of Scene 2.)

Scene 3

Lights up immediately at stage left. Scene is set as it was in Act I, set up during foregoing scene. SALLY *sits at the table as we left her.* MOTHER *enters speaking loudly and* SALLY *is startled.*

MOTHER: Did you get the table cleared, Sally? *(Notices that she hasn't done it)* Now move that wrapping business so I can put these dishes in place. We've got to hurry. (JANE *and* TOM *follow her in.*)

TOM: I'll be the best-dressed shepherd who ever watched sheep. Ugh!

JANE: Here's my collar, Mother. See? I found it. *(To* SALLY*)* Where's your angel stuff?

(SALLY *and* MOTHER *are busy with the table. As she speaks,* SALLY *reaches out to set a place and her arm is in front of* JANE, *who stands beside the table.*)

SALLY: It's ready. I'll get it in a minute.

JANE: Well, don't forget to take off that silly bracelet before the pageant. *(Holds up* SALLY's *arm)*

TOM: Hey! Where'd you get a grapevine bracelet? Somebody make it for you?

(All look at SALLY. *She stares at the bracelet and then looks up. Actors freeze. Lights out. End of Scene 3.)*

Scene 4

During scenes 2 and 3, JOSEPH, MARY, *and baby Jesus are present at center stage.* JOHN MARK *moves to stage right of manger. Lights up at center stage. Add lights on two side stages and families look toward center. All focus on the manger except* JOHN MARK.

JOHN MARK: *(Softly)* The greatest miracle in history. The Incarnation. The New Covenant. God's promise kept. *(Turns toward manger. All chronological line people, who have also remained on stage sitting or standing, focus on the manger.)* The greatest miracle!

ENTIRE CAST: *(Softly)* The greatest miracle!

(Lights out.)

THE END

Sets and props are simple. **Running time: 45 minutes.**

Abingdon Press